A CODE QUEST
ADVENTURE

MONMEORI · MONMEORI

Atlantis

Written by Mary-Jane Knight

Illustrated by Philip Chidlow

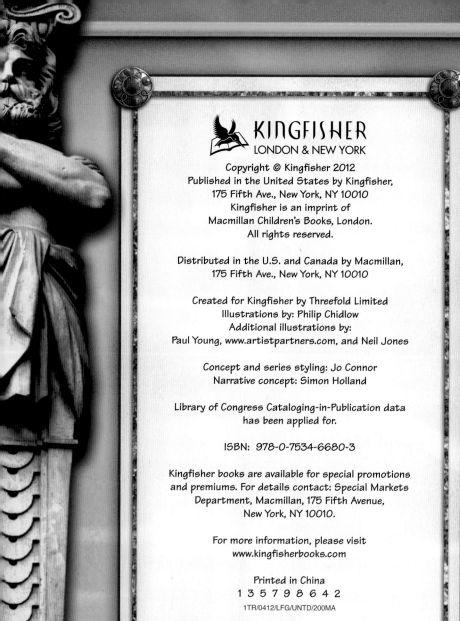

KINGFISHER
LONDON & NEW YORK

Copyright © Kingfisher 2012
Published in the United States by Kingfisher,
175 Fifth Ave., New York, NY 10010
Kingfisher is an imprint of
Macmillan Children's Books, London.
All rights reserved.

Distributed in the U.S. and Canada by Macmillan,
175 Fifth Ave., New York, NY 10010

Created for Kingfisher by Threefold Limited
Illustrations by: Philip Chidlow
Additional illustrations by:
Paul Young, www.artistpartners.com, and Neil Jones

Concept and series styling: Jo Connor
Narrative concept: Simon Holland

Library of Congress Cataloging-in-Publication data
has been applied for.

ISBN: 978-0-7534-6680-3

Kingfisher books are available for special promotions
and premiums. For details contact: Special Markets
Department, Macmillan, 175 Fifth Avenue,
New York, NY 10010.

For more information, please visit
www.kingfisherbooks.com

Printed in China
1 3 5 7 9 8 6 4 2
1TR/0412/LFG/UNTD/200MA

MONMEORI

4 MEET AMY JAMES
How to use this book

6 ATLANTIS: REALITY OR MYTH?
Step into the past

8 EXPLORING UNDERWATER
Step into the past

10 FIRE ONBOARD!
Follow the story

12 WE STRIKE A DEAL
Follow the story

14 WHERE TO START?
Solve the codes

16 MAPPING THE WORLD
Step into the past

18 THE MALTA CONNECTION
Follow the story

CONTENTS

20 NAMES AND NUMBERS
Solve the codes

22 MYSTERIES OF THE LABYRINTH
Follow the story

24 LEGENDS OF CRETE
Step into the past

26 THE ROAD TO ATLANTIS
Solve the codes

28 ONWARD TO THE ISLANDS!
Follow the story

30 THE SHAPE OF THE PAST
Solve the codes

32 UNDERSEA SEARCHERS
Step into the past

34 THE STORM
Follow the story

36 THE BROKEN ISLAND
Solve the codes

38 THE CITY BENEATH THE SEA
Follow the story

40 GLORIOUS RUINS
Solve the codes

42 FOUND AND LOST
Follow the story

44 THE LEGACY OF ATLANTIS
Step into the past

46 INDEX
Where to find things

48 THE SOLUTIONS
Check your answers

My name is Amy James, explorer. I need you to help me piece together some important clues. Together, we will try to figure out the location of a long-lost, sunken city . . .

MEET AMY JAMES

March 10, 1885

Dear code breaker,

My father was a sailor and explorer who left me an old leather bag of mementos. There's a piece of coral, a broken ship's compass, a few fragments of pottery, a tattered journal stuffed with old papers and maps, and a strange wheel with mysterious letters on it.

The journal is full of notes about a place my father called Atlantis. There are some scribbled phrases in strange letters in the journal and on the maps, which he refers to as Atlantean. Could this be a lost language?

My father thought he had glimpsed the lost city of Atlantis deep beneath the ocean. His ship ran aground on that trip, and for years afterward he tried to find the sunken city again.

He did not return from his last voyage but left instructions that I should be sent his bag.

Look out for evidence in each exciting scene.

*I've studied his journal, maps, and notes about Atlantis and know it is my destiny to continue the search. I'm about to stow away on the **Neptune**, a strange new boat that has been built here in Connecticut . . .*

Here is your challenge: read my story and look at all the clues and evidence I have found. Can you translate the mysterious messages, break the codes, and solve the mystery with me?

It is easy to miss something that could reveal a vital clue!

4

HOW TO USE THIS BOOK

As you read through the book, you will see exciting scenes from my adventure. Often, these are followed by "code-breaker" pages, in which I set out all of the clues for you to study. Code panels (the first is on this page) will show you the key codes in the story and tell you what you need to do to crack them.

As well as using the code wheel to translate the Atlantean code, you will find other puzzles and problems to solve. It would be a good idea to have a pencil and paper handy for making notes.

THE SOLUTIONS

If you get stuck on a clue or puzzle, take a quick look at page 48, where all the answers are given and explained.

But no cheating! The harder you try to solve them yourself, the more you will learn about code breaking and puzzle solving. Who knows, you might even find a few clues to the truth about what happened to the lost city . . .

THE CODE WHEEL

When you need to translate the Atlantean code, simply turn the wheel so that the big arrow with a hole in it points at the symbol you need to translate. Do this with each symbol in turn to find the hidden letters.

TIP: try to remember what common words such as "is," "and," or "of" look like in Atlantean. This will help you speed through the translations!

CLUE ONE:
THE LOST LANGUAGE

Nobody knows what Atlantean sounded like—the language has been dead for thousands of years. But using my father's notes and code wheel, I found a way to translate the jumble of symbols and letters into recognizable words.

Use the code wheel to translate this fragment of text. One of the words is very important, and you will see it often on your quest. Save time by remembering how it looks, so that you won't have to decode it every time.

MONMEORI RI M

CREYTGW GL

BGXEONUII RINUI

Amy's quest is to hide away on the Neptune *so she can be part of the hunt for the lost civilization of Atlantis. But did Atlantis ever exist, and if so, where?*

ATLANTIS: REALITY OR MYTH?

WHAT WAS ATLANTIS?

The story of Atlantis was written down hundreds of years ago, in about 350 B.C. An ancient Greek named Plato (below) wrote about a huge island in the Atlantic Ocean. From there, people called Atlanteans ran a great empire, which ruled over large areas of land and sea.

Stone bust of Plato

WHAT WAS ATLANTIS LIKE?

Plato said that Atlantis was built in the shape of a bulls-eye (below). A palace in the middle was surrounded by five rings of water and land. There were fountains with both hot and cold water, stone walls covered with precious metals, and huge statues made of gold.

A HUGE ARMY

Plato believed that Atlantis had a great army of more than a million soldiers. He claimed that the army had thousands of chariots, as well as foot soldiers armed with slings and javelins. The Atlanteans also had a navy of 1,200 ships.

Horse-drawn chariot

WHERE WAS THE STORY FROM?

Plato heard about Atlantis from a Greek traveler named Solon. He had heard the story from the ancient Egyptians. Even today, nobody knows whether the story was true.

The yellow spots on this map show possible sites of Atlantis in the Mediterranean Sea.

LOOKING FOR ATLANTIS

For hundreds of years, people have tried to figure out more about Atlantis, whether it was a real place, and where it might have been. People have written books and made movies about it. Some have suggested that Atlantis might have been in the Bahamas or the Caribbean, both in the Atlantic Ocean. Even the Antarctic has been suggested. Many now agree that the site was probably in the Mediterranean Sea.

THE BERMUDA TRIANGLE

Some people think that there may be a connection between Atlantis and a mysterious area of the Atlantic Ocean called the Bermuda Triangle. The triangle is not marked on maps, but it is often blamed for the disappearance of dozens of ships, planes, and people. The area is near the southeastern coast of the United States and is also known as the Devil's Triangle.

The Bermuda Triangle covers more than 386,000 sq. mi. (1,000,000km^2).

WHAT HAPPENED TO ATLANTIS?

Plato wrote that Atlantis had been destroyed by huge earthquakes and floods. He wrote that, in the space of a single day and night, everything sank into the earth and then disappeared into the depths of the sea. The island was never seen again, but people have been searching for it ever since.

Undersea earthquakes can cause huge waves called tsunamis (left).

To search for the lost city of Atlantis, people need to be able to explore the depths of the oceans, where perhaps the ruins of the city still lie . . .

EXPLORING UNDERWATER

EARLY DIVERS

The first divers may have been Assyrian soldiers who blew air into animal skins to help them breathe when they were crossing rivers. The first diving bell was invented in 333 B.C. It was like an upside-down jar, which trapped a pocket of air when it was lowered into the water. Divers took breaths of air from the bell instead of swimming to the surface.

Assyrians swam along with air-filled animal skins.

SUBMARINES THROUGH THE AGES

The first submarines were built about 500 years ago, and inventors gradually improved them as time went by.

1776 American David Bushnell built the first submarine to attack an enemy warship. It was called the *Turtle*, and it attacked a British ship in New York City Harbor.

1800 American Robert Fulton built a submarine in France called the *Nautilus*. It dived to depths of nearly 30 ft. (10m) for up to four hours.

Robert Fulton's Nautilus submarine

David Bushnell's Turtle submarine

1855 A submarine built for the Russians by Wilhelm Bauer made 134 dives. The most famous dive was to celebrate the crowning of Tsar Alexander II. The sub carried 16 men, including a brass band.

1900 The U.S. Navy launched its first submarine, called the U.S.S. *Holland*. It was armed with torpedoes and a deck gun.

1914–1918 Great Britain, France, Russia, Germany, and the United States all had subs during World War I. They launched torpedoes at enemy ships.

1918 Sonar (left) was developed. This sound system uses echoes to show where a submarine is underwater.

1939–1945 Submarines played an important part in World War II.

1954 The United States launched the U.S.S. *Nautilus*, the first nuclear-powered submarine. It could stay underwater for two weeks at a time.

1960 Jacques Piccard and Don Walsh set a world record when they went down to 35,797 ft. (10,911m) under the Pacific Ocean in the *Trieste*, a special submarine known as a bathyscaphe.

1985 The remains of the famous liner R.M.S. *Titanic*, which sank in 1912 after hitting an iceberg, were found 12,470 ft. (3,800m) below the surface of the North Atlantic off the coast of Newfoundland, Canada.

The *Trieste*

PEOPLE UNDERWATER

In 1943, Frenchmen Jacques Cousteau and Émile Gagnan helped develop an Aqua-Lung, which automatically gave divers air. For the first time, divers could stay underwater for long periods. In 1962, Cousteau lived for seven days under 30 ft. (10m) of water in the sea off the south of France.

Jacques Cousteau

Aqua-Lung system

In 1979, Sylvia Earle, an American oceanographer, set a record when she walked on the seabed 1,250 ft. (380m) below the surface. She wore a pressurized suit to explore the bottom for two and a half hours.

Today, there is an underwater laboratory called Aquarius, near Florida, where scientists work under 65 ft. (20m) of water for ten days at a time. Inside are bunk beds, a shower and toilet, a microwave, and a refrigerator. The scientists even have air conditioning and computers linked to others on land.

Most of the world's ocean floor is unexplored.

THE DEEPEST SEA

The deepest point of any ocean on Earth is in the Pacific. It is called Challenger Deep in the Marianas Trench. The bottom there is 35,797 ft. (10,911m) below sea level. The Challenger Deep is named after the British survey ship *Challenger II*, which discovered this deepest point in 1951.

FIRE ONBOARD!

I was not a secret stowaway for long.
I'd ventured out for air when I saw a spiral of
smoke curling under a cabin door. Opening the
door, I saw that some papers had caught fire.
I threw my bag aside, grabbed a nearby pitcher
of water, and threw it on the blaze, quenching
the flames. As I turned to pick up my bag
and its scattered contents, I came face to
face with the captain.

Taking advantage of his astonishment, I darted
past him, but I ran right into a sailor following
close on his heels. He caught and held me firmly
while I babbled an explanation. The captain's eyes
were fixed on my bag and the papers I'd hastily
gathered up. He asked me to explain myself. It
quickly became clear that we had a quest in
common. The papers that had caught fire were
old maps and documents, not unlike the ones my
father had left me. We started to discuss them . . .

THE NEPTUNE
SHIP'S CREW ROSTER
Captain: Mr. Darius B. Calder
First officer: Mr. J. Williams
Navigator: Mr. E. Murchison
Purser: Mr. M. Hernandez
Chief engineer: Mr. B. Rawlings
Ship's cook: Mr. H. Schultz
Ship's doctor: Dr. E. H. Stempel
Medical assistant: Mr. V. O'Rourke
Chief rigger: Mr. S. Jackson
Boatswain: Mr. C. Sedgewick
Boatswain's mate: Mr. F. Levy
Quartermaster: Mr. H. Kessler
Coxswain: Mr. G. Carter
Able seamen: 14
Total crew: 27

WE STRIKE A DEAL

The captain and I talked for hours, growing more excited as we realized that our purpose was the same—to find the lost city of Atlantis. We had countless descriptions of the place in my father's papers and in documents the captain had collected. Luckily, the fire had destroyed only a few, and the most important nautical maps and charts were safely stowed away. He was very grateful that I had put out the fire so quickly; otherwise it might have spread and destroyed the entire ship.

We agreed to share our maps and information in the hope of finding Atlantis together. With the help of the navigator, we concentrated on a map that seemed to offer more clues than any other. We decided that the most likely location was in the Mediterranean Sea and that there was a chance we might find further clues on the island of Malta.

As the Neptune *steamed noisily toward Malta, we examined the old maps and books for further clues. The more we looked, the more we found. I was convinced we were on to something . . .*

WHERE TO START?

A GOLDEN AGE?
In early times, many maps were drawn by Arabic navigators. They used complicated, crisscrossing lines to represent distance and direction. These accurate maps are now valuable treasures.

This old map has lines in gold ink that meet near Crete. We must investigate . . .

Crete

CLUE TWO:
THE SCROLL OF HADRAMAUT
We found a few words of Atlantean on this very old and fragile scroll. What could they mean?

LAGW TAUMT CMWRER

IKAREYI LRAU OG ZXUEBP

OU YNGAO GL MONMEORI

We noticed that one symbol appeared in several different places. This old book of maps has it on the cover. A clue to the secrets inside, perhaps?

CLUE THREE:
THE FAMILY OF ATLANTIS?

I found a phrase on a fragment of a map that had been rescued from the fire in the cabin. I excitedly showed it to the captain. Unfortunately, part of it was burned away.

ᗅᑌ ᗅᗅᑌᑌ ᕍᖇᑎᑕᗅᑌᕍ ᘜᒪ
ᗰᐱᑎᗰᕍᐱᖇᓮ ᕍᗅᖇᓮᐱᖇᗰᕍᖇ
ᗰᓮᗷᗰᕍᖇᗰ ᑌ . . . ?

It is becoming easier to recognize Atlantean writing.

The scene on this golden brooch (below) shows a ship passing grand buildings on small islands. Does this image represent Atlantis?

There are ancient, carved stone heads on a few of the islands in the Aegean Sea. Could these be the heads of Atlanteans?

A VIEW OF THE PAST

Jewelry in ancient times often depicted the lives of the people who created it. Looking at artifacts such as this brooch helps us find out about people's beliefs and the world they lived in, what they grew, and what they traded.

CLUE FOUR:
THE MYSTERY DEEPENS

The code wheel was proving to be extremely useful. On its reverse, I found some Atlantean letters scratched around the edge. Was this another clue left by my father?

ᗅᑌ ᓮᑌᗰᑎ ᖇᓮ
ᗅᑌ ᑕᑌᕦ

By now, we know that ᗅᑌ means "the," so our translations can start to speed up.

People have used maps to mark the positions of places for hundreds of years. Over time, as explorers returned from their voyages, newly discovered lands were added, and maps became more and more accurate.

MAPPING THE WORLD

FINDING THE WAY
Before compasses were invented, sailors figured out where they were by looking for landmarks and noting the position of the sun and the stars. Ancient mariners often stayed within sight of land so they did not get lost.

EARLY NAVIGATORS
The first people to navigate at sea were probably the Phoenicians, in about 2000 B.C. Sailors used charts and figured out directions according to the position of the sun and the stars.

Phoenician traders approach a wary tribe on the North African coast.

Rotating metal rings allow the compass to stay level as the ship moves around on the water.

An astrolabe helped sailors find out their latitude by measuring the position of the sun at noon.

NORTH, SOUTH, EAST, AND WEST

To find out where they were, sailors needed to know their latitude, or how far north or south they were. They also needed to know their longitude, or how far east or west they were. Both are measured in degrees, using the "°" symbol (see below).

Today, longitude is measured from the prime meridian, which runs through Greenwich, England, as shown on this old map (right). Places east of the prime meridian—such as India—have longitude angles up to 180° (degrees) east. Places west of the prime meridian—such as North America—have angles up to 180° (degrees) west.

NORTH AMERICA

equator

India

prime meridian

west

east

HOW FAST?

In the 1500s, sailors figured out how to measure the speed of a ship. They knotted a weighted line along set sections and let it out over the stern when the ship was underway. A sailor counted the knots that went out in a certain time to calculate the speed. Ship speeds are still measured in "knots." A knot is one nautical mile per hour (the same as 1.15 mph, or 1.85km/h).

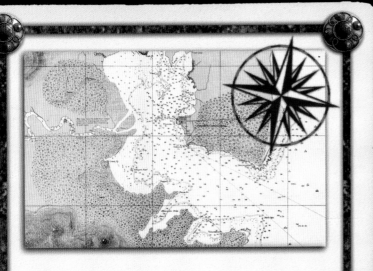

MAPS OF THE SEA

Maps that show seas and oceans are called nautical maps or charts. They show how deep the water is in different places so that boats do not run aground. The first charts were drawn during the 1200s. They were not very accurate, and they did not show lines of latitude or longitude, but a compass showed which way to travel.

Today, replica sailing ships remind us of the history of ocean navigation.

THE MALTA CONNECTION

Several days later, we docked in Malta and set out in search of further clues. Our first stop was a small, private museum near the harbor. Leaving the crew to restock the *Neptune*, we set off with high hopes. We spent hours looking through the amazing collection. There were ancient Greek pots and tiles, Egyptian paintings and statues, and Minoan frescoes (wall or ceiling paintings) and jewelry. But by the evening, we hadn't found anything that might be a clue.

✚

As we were thanking the charming owner, I spotted something in the library that sent shivers of recognition down my spine—it was a stone disk, with letters and symbols around its edge that looked very similar to the ones on my father's wheel. The museum owner kindly allowed us to make a clay impression (copy) of the disk to take away with us.

As we pored over all the material we had assembled, from my father's notebook to the artifacts we had found in Malta, some answers began to suggest themselves . . .

NAMES AND NUMBERS

CLUE FIVE: DISK DECODED

This stone disk was in the private collection we visited in Malta. After careful study, we found a sequence of letters around the edge. Some of the letters are too worn to read. The curator was kind enough to allow us to make an impression of the disk by rolling it along a strip of clay like a wheel. This is what was written:

BAMEMU OG AU HUIO .

UMIO NRUI BMAKMAXI .

AU YGNTUE HMNNI

MAU FXO (+L)

NUMYXUI LAGW AU

IMBAUT RINU

Part of the ruins of ancient Knossos, on Crete.

"C" IS FOR CHANGE

Many islands in the Aegean Sea have had different names over the centuries, and the spelling of some has changed, too. Karpathos was once called Carpathus; Kefallonia used to be Cephalonia; and Kos was Cos. So be aware of this when translating island names.

Among my father's notes is some Atlantean writing . . . He doesn't seem to have translated it, and there's no clue as to its origin. Some of the symbols are not on the code wheel, so was he was waiting to find more clues? I think the symbols in parentheses are numbers . . .

MONMEORI AUMEUI (+L‹) NUMYXUI OG WOCGEGI . (L+II) NUMYXUI OG BAMENU . OG MEERI (L) NUMYXUI

Use the code wheel, together with the number key under the flap (right), to translate the complete message.

At the museum, we almost missed this: some Atlantean on an ancient plate . . . Does it reveal another clue?

TUNGI WGIⴲ HGAIPRKUT

ROYAL DOLPHINS

According to my father's notes, the king of Atlantis had pet dolphins. One half-finished translation reads:

THE BLUE DOLPHINS SWAM _ _ _ LEAGUES
FROM ACHNIS TO BE WITH THE KING

I now know the missing symbols translate into a number. What is it?

(Π)   (✝)   (I)

Seafaring people often worshiped dolphins. You can see many dolphin images in their paintings, jewelry, and other crafts.

CODE BREAKER

Were we about to discover the site of the fabled lost kingdom at last? I knew it was important to figure out how the Atlanteans counted. I had a hunch that their system was like the Romans', and now I had the proof . . .

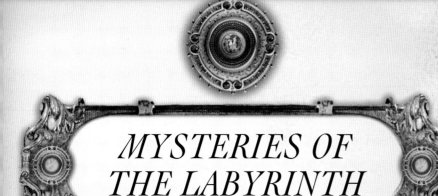

MYSTERIES OF
THE LABYRINTH

We were thrilled that we had found more clues and lost no time in setting out for the island of Crete, which was once the center of the Minoan civilization. We knew we might find further clues in the ruins of the Palace of Knossos. This was an enormous building with more than 1,000 rooms, built by the Minoans. It was destroyed, possibly by an earthquake or foreign invasion, in about 1700 B.C. and later rebuilt.

Our request to explore the ruins was met with a flat refusal from the official in charge. When asked why, he answered that the spirit of the Minotaur still roamed the labyrinth (maze), beneath the palace and we would not be safe. Unable to convince him otherwise, we retreated to the shade of a nearby tree. Here we waited until his attention was elsewhere and then sneaked in. My father had been here, and we followed a plan he had drawn in his journal, which took us down a shady avenue.

Heading north, we came to an overgrown
archway marked with an "X." Behind the vines,
we saw a dark opening. We entered cautiously,
feeling our way down a crumbling staircase to
a domed chamber. Weak rays of light filtered
through the cracks in the ceiling, fading as we
continued. Then the captain held up his lantern
to show us a passageway, which led into
darkness. Stone pillars stood on either side,
and peeling frescoes decorated the walls.
We gasped at the sight of the Minotaur
but were relieved to discover that it
was merely a bronze statue . . .

The searchers know that to unravel all the clues they've gathered, they need to find out more about the history of Crete and its people.

LEGENDS OF CRETE

CRETE LONG AGO

The people who lived on the island of Crete in the Mediterranean between about 2600 and 1150 B.C. are called Minoans. They were excellent sailors, and they traded with many countries, including Egypt and Mesopotamia. They sold wood, wine, fruit, wool, cloth, herbs, and olive oil. Minoan sailors also brought precious stones and metals, such as copper, silver, and gold, to the island.

This wall painting shows three Minoan women.

MINOAN CAPITAL

Knossos was the capital of Minoan Crete. Greek myths say that a man named Dedalus designed a great palace for the king, Minos. Minos wanted the palace to be so complicated that no one would be able to find the way out. He kept Dedalus prisoner so that the plans (right) would not be revealed. Dedalus cleverly built two sets of wings so that he and his son Icarus could fly away. But Icarus flew too close to the sun, and the wax that held his wings together melted, and he fell into the sea below.

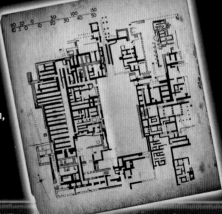

Icarus falling from the sky

THE LEGEND OF THESEUS AND THE MINOTAUR

Another Greek myth tells of how King Minos kept a horrible monster called the Minotaur—half bull, half man—in a labyrinth, or maze, under his palace. Every nine years, King Aegeus of Athens sent seven boys and seven girls to Crete to be eaten by the Minotaur.

One year, Aegeus's son Theseus offered to go. He told his father that he would kill the Minotaur and end the terror. His father begged him not to, but Theseus set sail with the other young Athenians.

When they arrived, King Minos's daughter Ariadne fell in love with Theseus and helped him. She gave him a sword and a ball of string to unwind as he walked through the maze, so he could find his way out again. Theseus found his way to the middle and killed the monstrous beast. He followed the string back to the entrance and found Ariadne and the others waiting. They ran to their ship and sailed away.

Theseus defeating the Minotaur

WHAT HAPPENED TO THE MINOANS?

No one knows what happened to the Minoans. Their palaces and roads were destroyed in 1700 B.C., perhaps by an earthquake or by invaders. They rebuilt their way of life but gradually became less powerful. We do not know what happened to them after 1400 B.C.

The ruined palace at Knossos

The Minoans were the first people to build paved roads.

We had escaped from the labyrinth, glad that the Minotaur hadn't shown up! Clutching our discoveries, we headed back to the Neptune—with no idea of what our next move should be.

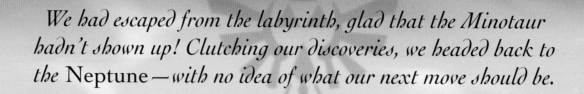

THE ROAD TO ATLANTIS

START

FINISH

THE PUZZLE OF THE LABYRINTH
Having correctly chosen the north door, we made our way to the center of the labyrinth. But finding the right path still proved to be difficult. Can you find our route to the treasure?

MAZES OF EGYPT
Greek legend tells us that there was an impressive labyrinth on the island of Crete. This was not the first, though—ancient Egyptians were building labyrinths 4,000 years ago. One of these is thought to have been 100 times bigger than the one on Crete!

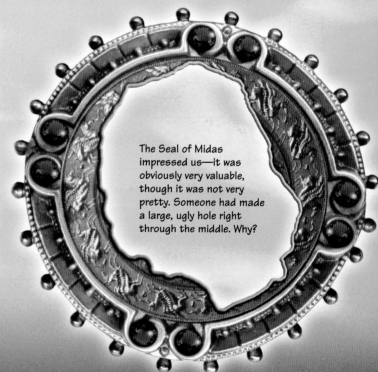

The Seal of Midas impressed us—it was obviously very valuable, though it was not very pretty. Someone had made a large, ugly hole right through the middle. Why?

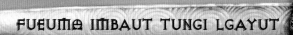

FUEUMA IMBAUT TUNGI LGAYUT

CLUE SEVEN: THE ANCIENT SWORD

We had found a sword in the labyrinth, with some Atlantean words etched into its blade. If we could translate these, they might lead us to the elusive island.

The sword was made of bronze, with a handle decorated in gold thread.

The crew worried that the sword might bring us bad luck, so we left it in the labyrinth.

ƎU BMXIUHMΘ

LAGW UIƏMOR AXƎI

ΘG MONMƎΘRI

MΘ AUIΘ

CLUE NINE: TINY ISLANDS

Many of the smaller Aegean islands, or islets, are often missing from historical maps. As we mused over our finds and translations, the captain remembered seeing a group of tiny islets on an old Maltese map. The names of the first two islands match the clue from the burned fragment (see page 15).

CLUE EIGHT: A COURSE REVEALED?

Along with the seal and the sword, we picked up some scrolls from the labyrinth. Among them was one decorated with images of the Minotaur. The Atlantean text might prove to be very, very important . . .

ƎU BMXIUHMΘ LAGW
UIƏMOR AXƎI ΘG
MONMƎΘRI MΘ AUIΘ

*We had made progress! The discoveries we'd made
in the labyrinth had given us a much-needed boost.
I settled into my bunk for some long-overdue sleep as
the Neptune set sail for the Aegean Sea . . .*

ONWARD TO THE ISLANDS!

After solving some of the clues we'd found in Crete, we lost no time in setting sail again.
Once we reached the open sea, the captain ordered a test dive. *Neptune* descended slowly to the murky depths, and it struck us how little we could see through the portholes. We needed to plot our course carefully and with great accuracy if we were to succeed in our quest. Once more, we turned to our collection of documents in search of further clues.

As I studied my father's papers, I noticed his habit of jotting notes at the edges or randomly on maps when a thought struck him. I worked my way through these notes, which were often difficult to make out. Suddenly, a sentence in Atlantean script leaped out at me. Beneath it was a translation. But it was wrong! As I reached for the code wheel, I wondered . . . could this be the final clue that would lead us to Atlantis?

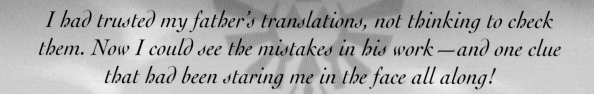

I had trusted my father's translations, not thinking to check them. Now I could see the mistakes in his work —and one clue that had been staring me in the face all along!

THE SHAPE OF THE PAST

MONMEORI ¥REUI FULGAU

BAMEMU HMCUI

This has me very confused. Perhaps the translation is a riddle? Maybe Amy can help me—she's good at puzzles.

MISTAKE IN THE TRANSLATION
No wonder it looked wrong. With the right words in front of me, I was struck by an idea . . .

MONMEORI ¥REUI
FULGAU BAMEMU HMCUI

GRÆCIA

CLUE TEN:
WEST TO EAST
Maybe the sun symbol was part of the clue. We know Cranae is also named Cythera, or Kythira. Perhaps the riddle meant Atlantis was east of Cranae, as the sun rises from the east. Of course, the first island that lies east of Cranae is Thera . . .

Thera

CRETICUM

If Atlantis was built on Thera, it would have been well placed to control the Aegean Sea.

At last we had discovered a likely site for the lost city of Atlantis. Excitement spread throughout the ship as we set a course for Thera. But little did we know that we would encounter another obstacle—a violent storm in our path. Would the Neptune be able to withstand the power of the elements?

CLUE ELEVEN:
A MISSING PIECE?
We wondered whether the odd shape in the middle of the Seal of Midas (see page 26) might be the outline of an island. Nothing on our maps seemed to match it.

Then I remembered my father's map of Santorini (also known as Thera). On the map, he had drawn the outline of the island as it might have been before the volcanic eruption destroyed it. It fit perfectly beneath the seal!

WHAT'S IN A NAME?
Santorini isn't the official name of Thera. Thera is the name of the largest of the islands that, as a group, share the name Santorini. Other islands in the group are Palea Kameni and Nea Kameni.

CLUE TWELVE:
AN ANCIENT RESCUE MISSION?
My father thought that Atlanteans who had been away when the city was destroyed may have returned to try to salvage their possessions. He found evidence—Atlantean words on a crumbling wall painting—to back up this idea.

ꕕU ꓟONꓟEꝋUꓟEI GL CEGIIGI ꝋG ꕕUAꓟ IꓟRNUT

31

*At last—the searchers feel that they are close
to solving the clues that might lead them to Atlantis.
How do today's underwater explorers travel?*

UNDERSEA SEARCHERS

LOOKING FOR SHIPWRECKS

A submersible is a boat built for underwater exploration. Many submersibles have arms and scoops that collect samples from the seabed. Some carry people, and others have cameras and lights to record what they find. In 1985, the wreck of the famous ocean liner *Titanic* was found by Robert Ballard in a manned submersible.

A Minoan ship design

An archaeologist studies an ancient Minoan shipwreck.

Robert Ballard finding the Titanic

A MINOAN SHIPWRECK

In 1976, the underwater explorer Jacques Cousteau found some Minoan pottery under the sea near the Mediterranean island of Pseira. Later, a Cretan diver named Elpida Hadjidaki found hundreds more Minoan containers there, including amphorae (types of jars), cooking pots, pitchers, and cups. Experts think that they come from the first wrecked Minoan boat ever discovered.

A Minoan amphora found at the shipwreck

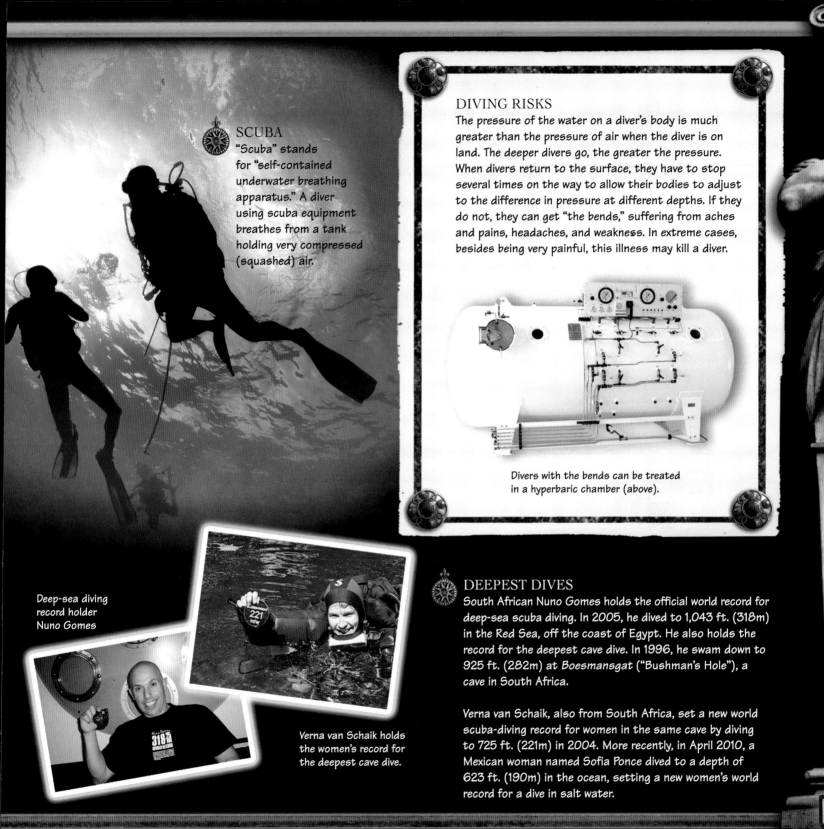

SCUBA

"Scuba" stands for "self-contained underwater breathing apparatus." A diver using scuba equipment breathes from a tank holding very compressed (squashed) air.

DIVING RISKS

The pressure of the water on a diver's body is much greater than the pressure of air when the diver is on land. The deeper divers go, the greater the pressure. When divers return to the surface, they have to stop several times on the way to allow their bodies to adjust to the difference in pressure at different depths. If they do not, they can get "the bends," suffering from aches and pains, headaches, and weakness. In extreme cases, besides being very painful, this illness may kill a diver.

Divers with the bends can be treated in a hyperbaric chamber (above).

Deep-sea diving record holder Nuno Gomes

Verna van Schaik holds the women's record for the deepest cave dive.

DEEPEST DIVES

South African Nuno Gomes holds the official world record for deep-sea scuba diving. In 2005, he dived to 1,043 ft. (318m) in the Red Sea, off the coast of Egypt. He also holds the record for the deepest cave dive. In 1996, he swam down to 925 ft. (282m) at Boesmansgat ("Bushman's Hole"), a cave in South Africa.

Verna van Schaik, also from South Africa, set a new world scuba-diving record for women in the same cave by diving to 725 ft. (221m) in 2004. More recently, in April 2010, a Mexican woman named Sofia Ponce dived to a depth of 623 ft. (190m) in the ocean, setting a new women's world record for a dive in salt water.

THE STORM

The captain and I had been so intent on scanning our papers and charts that it came as a surprise when the first officer knocked on the cabin door with a storm warning.
Through the portholes, the sky loomed gray and threatening, blotting out the sun, and moody thunderclouds were forming on the horizon. Rain was pelting down, and a rising wind was whipping up great white caps on the waves.

The *Neptune* needed to dive—and fast—to wait out the worst of the storm under the sea. The captain gave the order, but the chief engineer rushed in to report problems with the airlocks. Some were jamming, despite repeated attempts to close them. As the engineer was talking, the *Neptune* began to jolt and swerve through the heavy seas. Racing to the pump room, the captain and I joined in the struggle to operate the machinery before we lost control of the vessel . . .

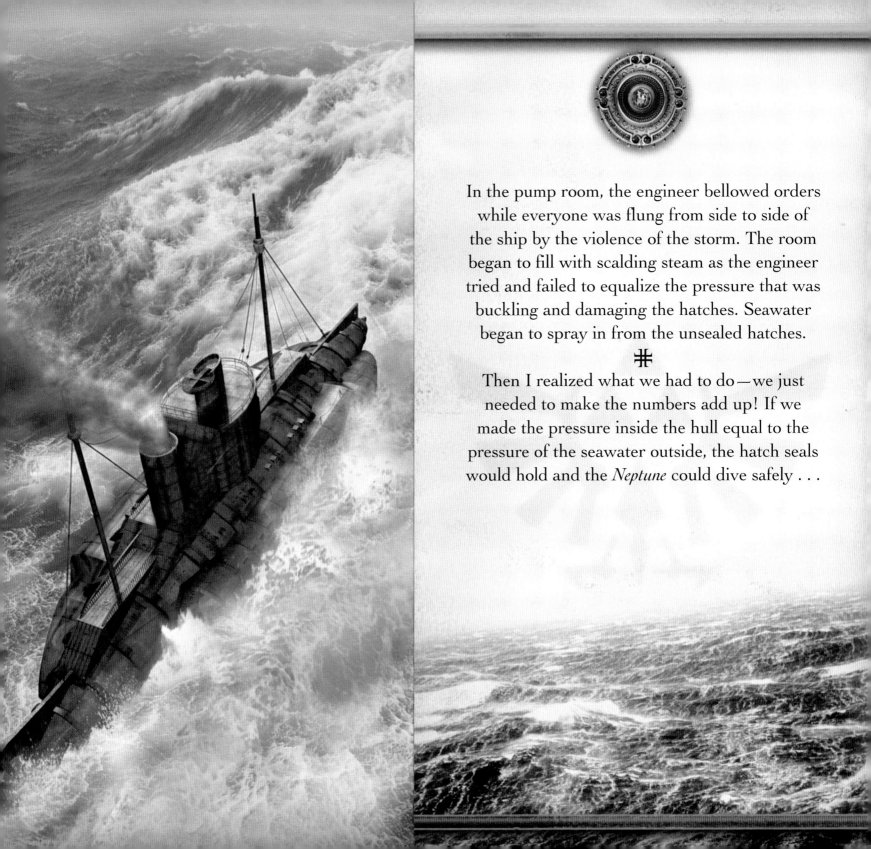

In the pump room, the engineer bellowed orders while everyone was flung from side to side of the ship by the violence of the storm. The room began to fill with scalding steam as the engineer tried and failed to equalize the pressure that was buckling and damaging the hatches. Seawater began to spray in from the unsealed hatches.

⌗

Then I realized what we had to do—we just needed to make the numbers add up! If we made the pressure inside the hull equal to the pressure of the seawater outside, the hatch seals would hold and the *Neptune* could dive safely . . .

The storm had passed, and we were very near Thera, but the Neptune was badly damaged. We had stopped sinking but could only drift helplessly until power was restored.

THE BROKEN ISLAND

THE DEPTHS OF THE AEGEAN SEA

East of Crete, the sea is as deep as 11,320 ft. (3,450m). Even the lagoon in the center of Thera is more than 1,310 ft. (400m) deep. Calypso Deep in the Ionian Sea, just west of Greece, is about 17,280 ft. (5,267m) deep!

There are some ruins in the channel.

CLUE THIRTEEN: MYSTERY ISLAND

Among my father's pictures was this print. An Atlantean phrase had been hastily copied on the back:

ᛗᛟᚾᛗᛖᛟᚱᛁ ᚨᚢᛁᛟᛁ ᚺᛈᚢᚨᚢ
ᛖᚢᛗ ᚹᚢᚢᛟᛁ ᚲᛗᚾᚢᛗ

SANTORINI

Santo

Erini

Palea

Nea

Is. Kameni

APANOMEREA

Early maps were often richly decorated with nautical scenes and imaginary landscapes.

PINPOINTED

On an old map of the island, I found what I was looking for. Two names jumped out—Palea and Nea Kameni. Perhaps the ruins of Atlantis were in the channel between these rocky outcrops. If only we could get underway!

CLUE FOURTEEN:
THE LAST LABYRINTH

In my father's journal was a drawing of a maze. I had been unable to make sense of it earlier, but now I saw that it might help us navigate the rocky channels. Would we find Atlantis at last? The Atlantean words written on the back of the map (right) were very confusing . . .

ΘHRSΘ HⅢNNI GL
IΘGEU ¥REUI ΔU IⅩE

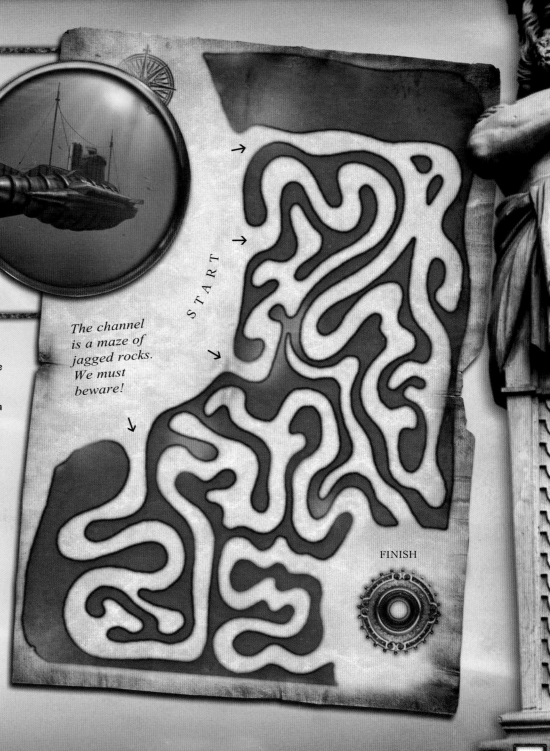

START

The channel is a maze of jagged rocks. We must beware!

FINISH

If the *Neptune* was unable to reach the underwater ruins that might lie between Palea and Nea Kameni, the captain said we would have to explore the seabed in specially made suits with big, metal helmets!

We could barely keep the submarine afloat. The crew worked feverishly, trying to get the Neptune safely back to the surface. The engines rattled and shook as we were drawn by strong currents deep into the rocky chasms . . .

THE CITY
BENEATH THE SEA

Finally we dived safely, but our submarine had been badly battered by the violent seas. As we descended, we realized that the steering gear was damaged and we could no longer control our direction. We watched helplessly through the portholes as the *Neptune* spiraled through the churning water.

As we dived deeper, the water became calmer and clearer—rocks loomed up and threatened us, but we were swept past the most jagged of them. Then I glimpsed the wreckage of a ship on the seabed, next to some broken pillars and huge blocks of stone. Excitedly, I pointed them out, and we made out part of the ship's name on the stern: *Perseus*. This was the last ship my father had been on . . . Glued to the portholes, we stared in wonder at the carvings on the pillars, which so closely matched the clues we had found. Shaken and stunned, we felt certain that these were the ruins of Atlantis!

We were deep under the towering cliffs of Thera. Through the portholes, we saw the shattered remains of a once-great city. There was no doubt in our minds — we had found Atlantis.

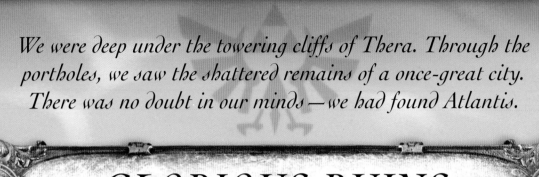

GLORIOUS RUINS

CAN YOU SEE IT?
We cannot see very far down into seawater, even when it is clear and unclouded. Strong sunlight reaches down to a depth of only 330 ft. (100m).

CLUE FIFTEEN:
A WARNING FROM THE DEEP
Some Atlantean letters were scratched into this carved stone. The graffiti artist seems to have had a premonition of the city's doom . . .

LRAU RI

BGWREY LNUU

@GXA PGWUI

THE DISK OF ATLANTIS
The Seal of Midas motif had appeared again and again during our quest. We were intrigued by what seemed to be four compass points. What did they represent?

Perhaps the seal was a plan of the lost city. As we passed through the ruins of Atlantis, we glimpsed a pair of columns that framed a portal (doorway) in the walls. There seemed to be intricate carvings on their surface . . .

Even the code wheel had the same seal pattern. Solve Clue Seventeen to discover what the compass points might represent.

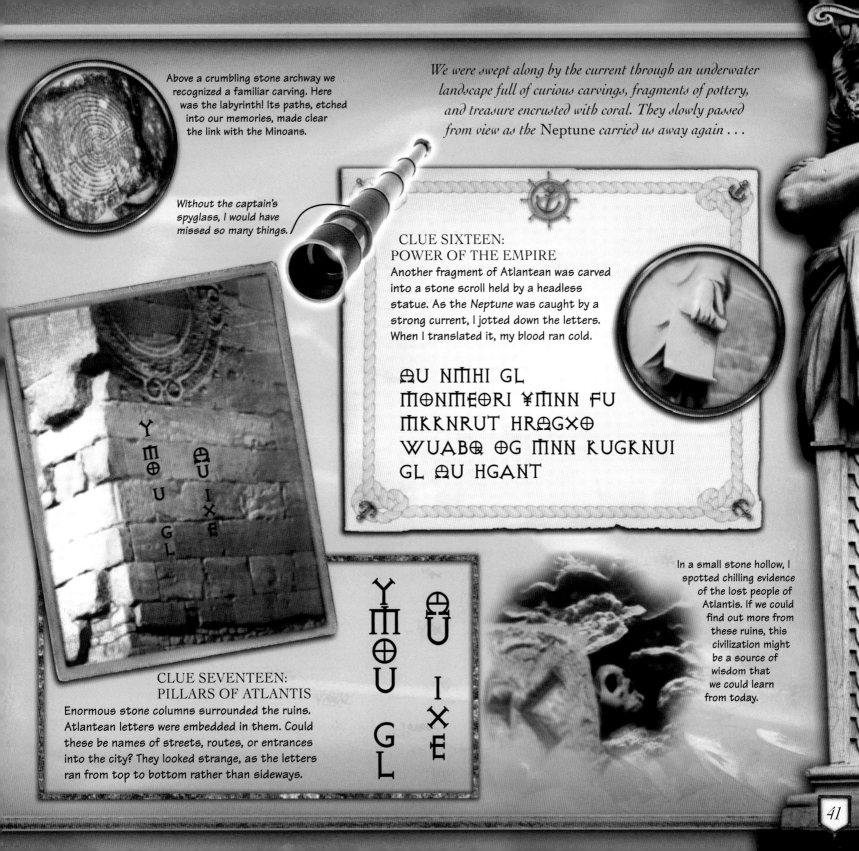

Above a crumbling stone archway we recognized a familiar carving. Here was the labyrinth! Its paths, etched into our memories, made clear the link with the Minoans.

We were swept along by the current through an underwater landscape full of curious carvings, fragments of pottery, and treasure encrusted with coral. They slowly passed from view as the Neptune carried us away again . . .

Without the captain's spyglass, I would have missed so many things.

CLUE SIXTEEN:
POWER OF THE EMPIRE
Another fragment of Atlantean was carved into a stone scroll held by a headless statue. As the Neptune was caught by a strong current, I jotted down the letters. When I translated it, my blood ran cold.

AU NMHI GL
MONMEORI YMNN FU
MKKNRUT HRAGXO
WUABO OG MNN KUGKNUI
GL AU HGANT

In a small stone hollow, I spotted chilling evidence of the lost people of Atlantis. If we could find out more from these ruins, this civilization might be a source of wisdom that we could learn from today.

CLUE SEVENTEEN:
PILLARS OF ATLANTIS
Enormous stone columns surrounded the ruins. Atlantean letters were embedded in them. Could these be names of streets, routes, or entrances into the city? They looked strange, as the letters ran from top to bottom rather than sideways.

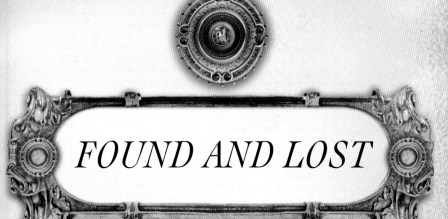

FOUND AND LOST

We were convinced that we had at last found the lost city of Atlantis. But there was no way of controlling the *Neptune*, and before long we were swept away from the ruins by the current. For a long while we drifted along the seabed, waiting out the storm above until it was safe to try to return to the surface.

Hours later, nearly suffocated by the stale air, we brought the *Neptune* back to the surface again. The storm had passed, but the chief engineer reported that he did not have the tools to repair the steering gear. We decided to stay on the surface until we could hail a passing ship. Sometime later we spotted an ocean liner, which threw us a line and towed us back to harbor in Crete. This stage of our quest was at an end, but the captain and I resolved that we would return and find the ruined city once more.

THE LEGACY OF ATLANTIS

THE ATLANTIS OF CONNEMARA

Many people have seen phantom islands in the Atlantic Ocean off the coast of Connemara in Ireland. Vinnie Delappe was 15 years old in 1972 when he saw the island. "I looked up and there, right in front of me, in the middle of the sea, was a real island . . . shimmering in the haze." Was this a sighting of Atlantis? Records of sightings go back for hundreds of years.

THE GIBRALTAR CONNECTION

In 2001, a French geologist named Jacques Collina-Girard suggested that Atlantis had once been a small island sitting in the Strait of Gibraltar. His theory was that Atlantis disappeared 11,000 years ago, when it was swamped by rising seas at the end of the last ice age.

EUROPE

Gibraltar

Spain

A possible site for Atlantis?

Strait of Gibraltar

Mediterranean Sea

ATLANTIC OCEAN

Ceuta (part of Spain)

Morocco

Tangier

AFRICA

This map shows how the sea level between the continents of Europe and Africa has risen over 19,000 years.

Land above sea level

Today

19,000 years ago

CLUES IN SOUTHERN SPAIN

In 2004, German scientist Rainer Kuehne thought that he had found the remains of the lost city in southern Spain. Satellite photos show rectangles in the mud with rings around them. These match Plato's description, and Kuehne suggests that the rectangles could be the remains of temples (below) devoted to the sea god Poseidon.

A village (above) in an area of salt marsh in southern Spain, which may be the site of the lost city.

A statue of the sea god Poseidon

This map (right) shows the possible shape of Atlantis.

Could this Google image, taken off the Canary Islands, show the street patterns of a lost city?

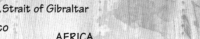

EUROPE

Spain

Mediterranean Sea

Strait of Gibraltar

Morocco

AFRICA

Canary Islands

ATLANTIC OCEAN

Atlantis hunters believe that the point where Africa, Europe, the Mediterranean Sea, and the Atlantic Ocean meet is very important in terms of locating the lost city.

ATLANTIS: FOUND ON THE INTERNET?

In February 2009, an engineer noticed a network of lines underwater—about 620 mi. (1,000km) off the coast of northwest Africa—while using online maps made by the Google Ocean project. Google's photos show that the rectangular area is about the size of Wales. Experts say that this sunken grid, which resembles a street system, is at one of the potential sites of the mythical city. But Google thinks the photos simply show lines made by their ship as it photographed the seabed in that area.

INDEX

A

Aegean Sea 7, 15, 30, 34

ancient Greeks 6

Antarctic 7

Aqua-Lungs 9

astrolabe 17

Atlantic Ocean 6, 7, 44, 45

B

Bahamas 7

Bermuda Triangle 7

C

Caribbean 7

compasses 4, 16, 17, 23

Crete 14, 20, 21, 22, 24, 25, 26, 28, 34

D

Dedalus 24

divers 8, 9, 32, 33

dolphins 21

E

earthquakes 7, 22, 25

F

floods 7

fountains 6

frescoes 18, 23

GHI

Gibraltar 44, 45

Icarus 24

islands 6, 7, 14, 15, 20, 31, 34, 44, 45

JK

jewelry 15, 18, 21

knots 17

L

labyrinths 22, 23, 26, 27, 41

latitude and longitude 17

legends (Greek and Minoan) 24, 25

M

Malta 12, 14, 18, 20

maps 4, 10, 12, 16, 17, 21, 27, 37

Marianas Trench 9

Mediterranean (region and sea) 7, 12

Minoans 18, 22, 24, 25, 26, 32, 41

Minos, King 24, 27

Minotaur 22, 23, 25, 26, 27

N

navigators 14, 16

MONMEORI

OP

Pacific Ocean 9

palaces 6, 22, 24, 25

Phoenicians 16

Plato 6, 7, 45

pottery 4, 18, 32, 41

QR

ruins 8, 22, 40, 41

S

ships 6, 7

shipwrecks 32, 38

soldiers 6

sonar 9

statues 6, 18, 41

submarines 8, 9, 11, 35

T

Thera 30, 31, 34, 40

Theseus 25

Titanic 9

treasure 41

tsunamis 7

UV

underwater exploration 8, 9, 32, 33

WXYZ

wall paintings 31

Picture credits & acknowledgments

Picture credits

The Publisher would like to thank the following for permission to reproduce their material. Every care has been taken to trace copyright holders. However, if there have been any unintentional omissions or failure to trace copyright holders, we apologize and will, if informed, endeavor to make corrections in any future edition.

(t = top, b = bottom, c = center, l = left, r = right): Pages 6cr, br Kingfisher Artbank; 8bc Kingfisher Artbank; 9cl, bc, br Kingfisher Artbank; 32br Shutterstock/ zeamonkey images.

3-D submarine modeling by Neil Jones

Acknowledgments

The Publisher would like to thank the following models:

Rob Armstrong (First Officer Williams)
Sarah Beaumont Bullock (Amy James)
Gareth Davies (crewmember)
Andrew Phillips (museum owner, page 19)
Laurence Walters (Captain Calder)